The Path to True Wealth

The Hidden Habits for Cultivating True Wealth and a Fulfilling Life

Elizabeth Wagner

Copyright © Elizabeth Wagner, 2024.

All rights reserved. No part of this publication may be reproduced, distributed, or transmitted in any form or by any means, including photocopying, recording, or other electronic or mechanical methods, without the prior written permission of the publisher, except in the case of brief quotations embodied in critical reviews and certain other noncommercial uses permitted by copyright law.

Disclaimer

The information provided in this book is for general informational purposes only. While every effort has been made to ensure the accuracy of the information contained within this book, the author and publisher assume no responsibility for errors or omissions, or for damages resulting from the use of the information contained herein.

This book is sold with the understanding that the author and publisher are not engaged in rendering legal, financial, medical, or other professional advice. The reader should consult with a professional in the respective field for any such advice.

TABLE OF CONTENTS

CHAPTER 1

True wealth extends beyond money

CHAPTER 2

How to cultivate an abundant mindset: Tips for thriving

CHAPTER 3

Tips for Building a Rich Inner Life

CHAPTER 4

Strengthen Relationships to Make Life More Beautiful.

CHAPTER 5

Steps to Live Your Life with Purpose

CHAPTER 6

Finding Meaning in Money: How to Live a Fulfilling and Purposeful Life

CHAPTER 1

True wealth extends beyond money

I feel that genuine riches entail much more than simply money. It's living life on your terms by gaining power, freedom, and confidence. When we speak about wealth, we feel it encompasses much more than just what is in your bank account.

Money is simply one aspect of life that counts. Living on your terms is having the flexibility to live your life as you see fit, following your hobbies, and making memorable moments with your loved ones. It's about being able to face life's challenges with confidence, knowing you're financially prepared for whatever comes your way.

In a world where success is often measured in monetary terms, it's important to remember that wealth is much more than the size of your bank account. I want to investigate the premise that money alone does not ensure real prosperity. Many people achieve great fortune, yet their lives are lacking in other important areas, such as relationships, health, and personal independence. The Illusion of Money as the Only Measure of Success. It is all too frequent to see individuals succeed financially while struggling in other aspects of their lives. While money is vital, it should not be prioritized above our health, relationships, or general well-being. True wealth is a comprehensive idea that goes beyond financial prosperity.

The Concept of True Wealth

True prosperity entails a balanced and fulfilled life. It includes not only financial success but also:

1. Health: Good health is the cornerstone of a prosperous lifestyle. Without it, no amount of money can purchase pleasure. Investing in your well-being is an essential component of genuine riches.

2. Relationships: Deep bonds with family, friends, and loved ones are invaluable. Building and cultivating these connections enriches and fulfills your life.

3. Time: True riches give you control over your time, not the other way around. Achieving a work-life balance and personal freedom are critical components of true success.

4. Mission: Discovering your life's mission and making a good difference in your community or across the globe is an essential component of riches. It extends beyond just gaining riches for personal advantage.

Key to Building True Wealth

Balance is key: Strive for balance in all areas of your life, not just finances. Remember that success has several dimensions. Prioritize Invest in your physical and emotional well-being. Without good health, riches lose their charm.

Cultivate connections: Take care of your connections and devote time to those who are most important to you. Strong relationships are a critical component of your wealth.

Time Management: Don't let money dominate your time; instead, strive for financial freedom so you can manage your time.

Find Your Purpose: Seek a feeling of purpose that extends beyond money. Making a difference in the lives of others may be very fulfilling.

CHAPTER 2

How to cultivate an abundant mindset: Tips for thriving

It's easy to get into a loop of wanting more—more money, success, and goods. We end up believing that what we have is never enough, trapping ourselves in a negative attitude of scarcity. Fortunately, there is another way to see the world and concentrate your attention on the plethora of chances and benefits that surround us. An abundant mentality is a life-changing strategy that may lead to increased happiness, contentment, and peace of mind.

What is the abundant mindset?

An abundant mentality holds that there is enough money, pleasure, and success in the world for everyone. It is a viewpoint that sees life's potential as infinite, urging us to tackle events and problems with hope and kindness. It's about perspective. An abundant mentality is characterized by a positive attitude toward chances rather than difficulties. When we adopt this attitude, we believe in development, change, and the possibility of great results, which may help to relax our brains during stressful situations. It inspires generosity. With an abundant mentality, we believe that giving our resources, time, and expertise creates a circle of generosity that benefits everyone. Recognizing and acting on the concept that giving to others may enhance both our own and others' lives contributes to the development of a feeling of community and connection. It encourages thankfulness.

An abundant attitude allows us to appreciate what we already have rather than focusing on what we lack. By consistently identifying and appreciating wealth in our lives, we create a greater feeling of satisfaction and happiness. It keeps us open to possibilities. Having an abundant mentality entails saying yes to life, accepting change, and being ready to move outside of our comfort zones to learn and develop.

This openness guarantees that we do not miss out on opportunities for personal growth and satisfaction. It keeps us optimistic and motivated. Above all, an abundant mentality is defined by the belief in limitless possibilities. It is the realization that there is always another opportunity, alternative, or course to take.

How to develop an abundant mindset: 8 methods to generate abundance.

Adopting an abundant mentality is a transforming experience that opens up a world of possibilities. These basic, practical ideas will help you live a more full life.

1. Change is inevitable, so why not embrace it? When confronted with new circumstances, strive to see them as opportunities to develop and learn. This method may help you navigate life with more comfort and less worry.

2. Let appreciation transform your mindset from scarcity to abundance. Practice thankfulness every day and make it a habit to reflect on what you're grateful for, whether it's family love, excellent health, or even minor delights like a bright day. This may radically alter your viewpoint, allowing you to notice the plenty around you.

3. Practice mindfulness and stay present. Instead of stressing about the future or obsessing over the past, concentrate on the present moment and appreciate what is wonderful around you. Mindfulness activities, such as meditation and deep breathing, may help you stay present in the moment, increasing your feeling of richness.

4. Celebrate other people's accomplishments. Joyfully applauding the accomplishments of others is a clear sign of an abundant attitude. When you celebrate someone else's accomplishments, it fosters the perception that success is limitless and there is enough to go around. This activity fosters a feeling of togetherness and shared delight, rather than competitiveness.

5. Identify and confront limiting beliefs. We all have limiting ideas that might prevent us from reaching our greatest potential. Recognizing these ideas is the first step in questioning and altering them. When you find yourself thinking negatively or questioning your talents, challenge them and replace them with positive affirmations that reflect an abundant attitude.

6. Be generous with others so that you may see your richness. Sharing your time, resources, and compassion with others not only helps others but also boosts your feeling of richness. When you give freely, you communicate to yourself and the world that there is enough to go around, and this generosity returns to you in a variety of ways.

7. Surround oneself with favorable influences. Our thinking is heavily influenced by the people and situations around us. Seek out good influencers, such as friends, family, and mentors, who have an abundant perspective. Their viewpoint and enthusiasm might motivate and inspire you to adopt a similar approach in your own life.

8. Set objectives and take action. Having an abundant mentality is thinking that you can attain your aspirations and goals. Set specific, attainable objectives and take persistent action towards them. This proactive approach

strengthens your conviction in the possibilities and your power to produce prosperity in your life.

CHAPTER 3

Tips for Building a Rich Inner Life

So, you want to create a full inner life, right? You've come to the correct location! In this part, I've included all of the information you need to nurture your soul, increase your self-awareness, and achieve genuine satisfaction inside yourself. Whether you're an experienced introspection or just beginning to examine the depths of your soul, these guidelines can help you on your path to a more meaningful and purposeful life.

Tips for Developing a Rich Inner Life

In today's fast-paced and chaotic environment, it's easy to get caught up in the daily grind and ignore our inner self. However, having a fulfilling inner life is critical to our general well-being and pleasure. Practice mindfulness, develop a regular meditation practice, cultivate gratitude, prioritize self-reflection, engage in self-care activities, seek meaningful connections, read books and explore new ideas, embrace solitude and silence, practice self-compassion, and express yourself creatively to deepen your connection with yourself and live a more fulfilling life.

1. Practice mindfulness. Mindfulness is the discipline of focusing your attention on the present moment with openness and curiosity. Daily mindfulness activities may help you develop a stronger sense of awareness and appreciation for the present moment. Begin by devoting a few minutes every day to focusing on your breath and observing any thoughts or feelings that occur without judgment. Regular practice will improve your capacity to remain present and lessen stress.

2. Establish a regular meditation practice. Meditation is a very effective strategy for improving your inner life. Set aside time each day to sit in meditation. Find a comfy, peaceful place where you will not be bothered. Experiment with various meditation approaches, such as focused concentration or loving-kindness meditation, to see what works for you. Regular meditation practice may help you develop a deeper feeling of serenity, clarity, and self-awareness.

3. Cultivate thankfulness. Gratitude is a transforming habit that may help you change your perspective and bring more pleasure and optimism into your life. Keep a thankfulness diary and jot down three things you are thankful for every day. Thank people for their compassion and assistance. Take some time to concentrate on the wonderful parts of your life, no matter how tiny. By practicing thankfulness, you will have a

stronger feeling of satisfaction and appreciation for the current moment.

4. Prioritize self-reflection. Self-reflection is essential for knowing yourself and your purpose in life. Schedule frequent self-reflection and introspection sessions. Ask yourself thought-provoking questions such as, "What are my values and how am I living by them?" or "What gives me joy and fulfillment?" Discover your hobbies, interests, and ambitions. Self-reflection allows you to develop a better knowledge of yourself and make more purposeful decisions in your life.

5. Practice self-care activities. Taking care of your physical and mental health is essential for developing a fulfilling inner life. Prioritize your physical health by exercising, eating healthy meals, and getting adequate sleep. Find activities that make you happy, relaxed, and peaceful. Set limits to preserve your health and emphasize self-care. Nurturing yourself will provide you with the energy and vigor needed to create a vibrant inner life.

6. Seek genuine friendships. Developing and cultivating connections with loved ones is critical to our happiness and inner contentment. Take the time to reconnect with your family and friends, develop those ties, and strengthen your feeling of connection and belonging. Join communities and organizations based on your

interests and beliefs. Engage in deep and meaningful discussions to connect on a deeper level. By pursuing meaningful relationships, you will enhance your inner world with the links you form.

7. Read books to discover fresh concepts. Books provide portals into many worlds and views. Reading across genres may introduce you to fresh ideas and ways of thinking, broadening your horizons. Explore many points of view and ideas, even if they contradict your own. By exploring new concepts, you will increase your knowledge and comprehension, allowing for personal development and a deeper inner existence.

8. embrace isolation and stillness. In today's hyper-connected society, stillness and alone have become uncommon commodities. However, these periods of silence and introspection are essential for developing a full inner life. Spend time alone, free from interruptions, and appreciate your own company. Engage in activities that encourage inner stillness, such as nature walks or yoga. Allow yourself to withdraw from technology and make time for profound contemplation in your inner world.

9. Practice self-compassion. Self-compassion is the discipline of being compassionate and understanding to oneself, particularly during times of difficulty or failure. Instead of languishing in self-judgment, it's crucial to

forgive yourself and learn from your errors. Treat yourself with the same care and understanding that you offer others. By practicing self-compassion, you will develop a stronger feeling of self-love and acceptance, resulting in a more fulfilled inner life.

10. Engage in creative expression. Creativity is an essential aspect of being human. Discover and nourish your creative outlets, whether it's writing, drawing, dancing, or playing a musical instrument. Allow yourself the space to honestly express yourself via creativity. Use it for self-expression and discovery. By participating in creative expression, you may explore your inner depths and find new aspects of yourself, resulting in a more vivid and rich inner existence.

Incorporating these principles into your daily routine will help you create a vibrant inner life. Remember that developing these habits and behaviors is a process that will take time. Be patient with yourself and accept the process. Ultimately, investing in your inner well-being will result in more contentment, pleasure, and a stronger connection with yourself and the world around you.

CHAPTER 4

Strengthen Relationships to Make Life More Beautiful.

One of the most powerful experiences we may have in life is our connection to other people. Positive and supportive relationships will make us feel healthier, happier, and more content with our lives. So, here are a few recommendations to help you build more good and healthy connections in all aspects of your life.

We all have connections. We have acquaintances, family, coworkers, neighbors, and perhaps some pals. However, for a big portion of us, many of these interactions are just unsatisfactory. They are unsatisfactory because they lack actual strength, which stems from a lack of real depth.

Unfortunately, in today's world, we have shallow, superficial interactions with people, and it is quite difficult for this kind of relationship to deliver much more than fleeting happiness. Based on my expertise as a communication and confidence coach, **I'd want to teach you how to add substantial depth, and hence strength, to your relationships and make your social life much more important.**

Develop a greater sense of trust. A long time ago, my brother and I debated whether love, trust, or desire were more vital in a relationship. I've learned, however, that trust is critical in every relationship. Years later, I purchased my brother a picture of a tiny girl smiling and looking boldly at the camera, with an elephant's foot just over her head.

The caption read: "To trust is more important than to love." That remark rings true to me since no love can continue without equal degrees of respect and trust.

Meet More People. The quality of the individuals you meet is strongly related to the number of people you encounter. If you don't know many people and just meet one or two new people every season, you will seldom meet people who are a good fit for you in terms of personality, interests, and values. And, since this natural connection is so important in developing good relationships, you will have few opportunities to do so.

Conversely, if you go out a lot, meet a lot of new people, and continually extend your social circle, you're far more likely to encounter individuals you'll get along with, and these people have a great chance of becoming wonderful friends, loyal partners, and so on. This is why meeting new people is so crucial. Use social networks such as Facebook, LinkedIn, and others to meet new people.

Listen carefully. Listening is an important ability for raising someone's self-esteem; it is a quiet type of flattery that helps individuals feel encouraged and respected. The most fundamental aspect of good contact is listening and comprehending what people say to us, and vice versa.

Give folks your time. Giving somebody your time is also a valuable gift. In a world where time is of the essence and we are attempting to squeeze in more than one lifetime, we do not always have time to devote to our loved ones, friends, and coworkers. Technology has reduced our capacity to establish genuine relationships, and we try to multitask by texting and chatting at the same time.

Being present in the time you offer to others is also crucial so that when you are with them, you are there and not focusing on the past or worried about the future. The connections we form with others are the foundation of our existence, and investing time, energy, and effort in creating and maintaining relationships is one of the most important life skills.

Discuss the Things That Matter To You. When two individuals learn they have the same beliefs and interests, their connection becomes stronger. These shared ideals and interests are what foster the closest emotional connection. I've seen that many individuals have in-depth chats. They speak about trivial things like the weather, what's on TV, and the lifestyles of different movie stars, but they seldom discuss what matters in life. This is a mistake in my opinion since it is the ideal approach for a relationship to not grow. Discuss the issues that are most important to you, and let people know what you care about and believe in. If they believe in and care about the same subjects, they will happily inform you. As a result, you will uncover important common ground and feel more connected.

Express weakness. Many individuals want to come off as flawless. They don't discuss their failures, conceal their flaws, and never say anything that would humiliate them. However, all of this is a cover-up. You may look ideal to others, but you are not, and they are also aware of this. You are simply human, and people have problems.

However, by disguising your shortcomings, you succeed in making yourself look cold and impersonal. You resemble a marble statue rather than a genuine person. And this makes it difficult for others to connect with you emotionally; people connect, not with principles.

Keep this in mind, and don't be scared to exhibit your vulnerability and humanity. This is what elevates a connection to the next stage.

Have integrity. Integrity, as I view it, is the alignment of your ideas, words, and deeds. Integrity is shown when you speak what you believe and follow through on your promises. This is an important characteristic because if you have integrity, others will trust you. They can trust you to provide honest criticism, even if it is difficult or superficial, and they can rely on you to meet your commitments.

Trust is a key component of a healthy relationship, both personally and professionally. So, no matter how difficult it is at times, strive to maintain your integrity. Be honest with those around you, even if it means they may be wounded at first. It is more vital for them to trust you than to avoid being wounded.

Always keep your promises. Even better, consider hard before making any promises, and only guarantee what you can and are ready to deliver.

Be There for Others. Another essential component of healthy partnerships is support. People's relationships strengthen when they can depend on each other for assistance when it is required, whether that support takes the form of a few nice words or numerous large deeds. Of course, you cannot be available to everyone at all times.

Your time, energy, and resources are limited. However, you can recognize the essential people in your life and make every effort to be there for them. Your assistance will aid them practically and soothe them emotionally; this makes a huge difference in a relationship.

Manage mobile technologies. Most individuals now own a cell phone, and many have two or more. While they are a lifeline in an emergency and a useful tool for communication, they can also be a total distraction when individuals display a lack of mobile phone etiquette.

Learn to offer and receive feedback. Feedback, in my view, is the nourishment of advancement, and although it may not always taste pleasant, it may be quite beneficial to you. The capacity to offer constructive criticism to others allows them to realize their full potential and may assist in fostering pleasant and mutually beneficial relationships. From your viewpoint, any comment you get is free information, and you have the option of accepting it or not. It might help you tap into your blind spot and acquire a new viewpoint.

Develop empathy. I discovered this excellent statement a long time ago: "People will forget what you said, what you did, but they will never forget how you made them feel." Empathy and understanding foster connections between individuals. It is the condition of detecting and responding to another person's emotions and needs without criticizing, offering advice, or attempting to resolve the problem.

Empathy also includes "reading" another person's inner condition and interpreting it in a manner that benefits the other person, offers support, and fosters mutual trust. Every interaction we have may teach us something, and creating healthy relationships with others can make us happier and more satisfied, as well as feel more supported, supportive, and connected.

You may strengthen and progress a broad variety of connections in your life by adopting the proper mentality and conduct. Strong connections make you feel not just more satisfied, but also more connected to the rest of the world. You feel like your life has genuine meaning, you have more joy, and you live in the present. A universe of possibilities opens up in front of you.

CHAPTER 5

Steps to Live Your Life with Purpose

How to pursue your passion and live in flow. Are you striving to build your ideal life or business? If so, you're most likely sidetracked by the "how." Identifying your calling should be your first emphasis. I know personally that nothing else matters if you are not living your soul's mission. Once you've identified it, you may drive all aspects of your life in that direction. It is possible to accomplish what you love while living in flow; all you need is the correct motivation, mentality, and action.

1. Understand what life should be like. "Living on purpose" refers to accomplishing what is important to you by your values and beliefs. I can't tell you what it means for you, but you'll know when you're feeling it — or not. When you're not being yourself, everything seems cloudy and drab. You are both bored and busy, and you are always fatigued. Even minor tasks seem like labor.

You take tests to figure out why you're down, and medicines to help you feel better. This list may go on. If you continue to disregard your higher self, it will give you nudges — even a smack in the face — to draw your attention. When you're in sync, life is good. Things are simple, and everything simply works. You feel lively, enthusiastic, and energized from the inside. You're not worried about how you'll get there; you're confident in yourself, even if you're afraid.

2. Discover your true calling. Stop looking outside of yourself for solutions. There is just one option: be who you were meant to be. There are several activities available online to help you determine your calling, but they are unnecessary. Deep down, you know what makes you feel alive. You only need to pay attention. Don't know what your purpose is? You'll be able to put it into words after you stop stressing about whether you're expressing it correctly or whether others "get it."

However, uncertainty may limit access to your soul, particularly if you've disregarded it for a long period. In such a scenario, try connecting with yourself and tuning in to what's hidden there by asking, "What do I need to know or listen to here?" Then believe the response. I believe that writing is the most effective method to do this, but you can also do it as part of meditation or while walking or driving.

3. Believe in yourself and disregard what others think. We are inherently perceptive before we learn "the rules." However, there is no right or wrong way to live. If you don't follow your gut, you're functioning on someone else's terms - and no one can teach you how to be yourself. There is always a different approach to

everything. I disliked creating marketing funnels until I began doing them my way. Visionary leaders act differently, which is why they stand out. They challenge the norm to discover what is best for them. Imagine you've achieved success. Nobody will challenge you since you are on top of the world. Who would you be? How would you react? Confidence and self-belief are essential. Make a conscious decision that you know what is best for you. Place your palm on your heart and remind yourself, "I trust my ability to make the best decisions for me." Do this for every key aspect of your life.

4. Feel your fear and take the first step nevertheless. If you don't get up enthusiastic to start your day, pull off the bandage. Make a shift or begin taking action. While keeping alignment requires practice, you don't have to strive forever to get it.

The unknown is frightening. We feel secure and comfortable with the way things have always been. Fear is a natural part of us and will always be there, but it cannot dominate you until you allow it to; thus, take action toward your objectives regardless. You do not need to know how or feel prepared or worthy. After years of struggle, I recognized I wasn't doing my soul work and traveled across the globe to start fresh with my family. With practically little money, I left myself no alternative but to achieve by pursuing my love for helping people. It paid off, and I've never looked back. While your route may not be as severe, you must take the first step.

5. Rethink your task list. Time is valuable, and you should consider how you use it. If you don't determine what's important ahead of time, you'll waste your time doing things that won't get you anywhere. I regularly describe my aims and ambitions in a paper titled "Creating the Life I Want." I make sure to define those objectives for myself (not others), identify the steps that will bring me there, and plan them each week. Imagine yourself a year from today, living with purpose. Is the items on your to-do list today important? Is this how you got there? Examine your list of tasks and decide whether to remove, complete, or assign them.

It is sometimes worthwhile to pay someone else to do things so that you may concentrate on what is important: the chores that, if completed every day, will bring you where you want to be. If you don't care enough about a goal to make regular progress toward it, it may not be as important as you believe. But if you want it, you'll put in the effort.

6. Schedule daily check-ins with yourself. Before you get out of bed in the morning, consider what is essential today. What might help you sleep better tonight? Most of what we do during the day disconnects us from

ourselves, so try tuning in. Simply sit or write whatever has to come out for 15 minutes. Let go and disregard the outside world, even if it means starting with the universe you've made for yourself. Before making a choice or taking action, ask yourself, "Do I want to do this?" Does this feel correct? Am I thrilled about this? Set reminders to check in regularly to avoid falling back into old habits.

7. Recognize that you already have all you need. This may be unpleasant at first, and it may sometimes seem like an effort. But when you're doing the right thing, it's worth it. You may either deny yourself or say yes to your heart and soul, but you get to pick what you want in life. Make the effort now to shape the future of your aspirations. If you believe that everything will work out, it will. Don't worry if you don't obtain the results you desire today.

Success takes time, which is why many individuals quit. You will never look back and say, "I spent too much time being myself," so keep going. It's impossible to fail at being yourself. You've got everything you need. When you know who you are, you will become the person you were born to be.

CHAPTER 6

Finding Meaning in Money: How to Live a Fulfilling and Purposeful Life

Money is seldom spoken in terms of positive, affirmative meaning. In truth, money is nothing more than a means to a goal; it is energy that must flow through the system to accomplish its intended function. It is not an end in itself. Many Americans seem to have linked their self-worth and value to financial possessions over the years, which has hurt our general emotional wellness.

Money is not only about the dollar symbol. The more money we have, the more we believe that money is about dollars and decimals. We are trained to believe that the more zeros and commas in our bank account, the greater our worth and value.

In actuality, **"True wealth"** is linked to our sense of purpose and fulfillment, which stems from our desire to contribute to something higher than and beyond ourselves. It may seem ludicrous to those of you reading this who have few "zeros and commas," but in my experience, those with "fewer commas" and "more contribution" appear to live with a greater feeling of fulfillment and pleasure. Those with great amounts of income who do not use their riches to assist others, rather than simply themselves, seem to suffer from despair, anxiety, and a general lack of purpose in their life. Money may be an effective weapon for change. Whether or whether you feel there is more to life than what we can buy with our money, financial resources may be an effective weapon for change. I've been privileged to serve and surround myself with incredible individuals who want to utilize their financial status to help others who are less fortunate.

One aspect of my practice that greatly inspires me is assisting those who have created or inherited financial wealth in shifting from a growth mindset to one of contribution; deepening their sense of purpose in life by learning how to deploy their wealth to serve others in a way that is meaningful to what they feel called to do in the world. This allows us to reconnect with the "true value" of money and spend it in ways that offer ourselves and others tremendous pleasure and plenty.

Live With Purpose.

If money is a means to a goal, what function does it serve? After we reach a certain level of wealth that allows us and our loved ones to live a life where all of our requirements are met and we have a suitable lifestyle, we can shift our focus to leveraging what we've earned to improve our service to others. There is a subconscious undercurrent that most of us seldom notice, yet it has a powerful propensity to reduce our sense of worth and value. That undercurrent is made up of all the instances of self-serving conduct in which we know we might have benefited others by using our abilities, riches, or connections to advance/support others while still advancing oneself. Aligning our activities with our beliefs and fuelling our conduct with good and mutually beneficial intentions has a significant impact on our feeling of purpose and contribution. Typically, the ultimate consequence is a greater sense of contentment and self-esteem.

Remember your values.

If your business is something you're enthusiastic about, such as cuisine, music, art, fitness, or sports, you're likely to already have some guiding principles, or a "true north" for your company. For example, do you feel you have a duty to do something good with your life and company, no matter how little or trivial it may seem to others? If that's the case, you're unlikely to abandon your quest due to its difficulty.

If you don't, you could be lying to yourself or you're in the wrong business. When it comes to personal values, believing in your abilities implies that you will not be swayed by external circumstances. You don't take it personally when things don't go as planned. You do your best, and if you don't "succeed," you improve or readjust to get your intended result. Here are some strategies to start living with purpose today. Most of us will achieve some amount of success in our lives, whether financially, professionally, or personally. This is particularly true if we are functioning from a higher purpose and want to serve something larger than ourselves. The challenge is to avoid being so focused on monetary riches that we lose sight of the meaning and purpose that money may help us create in our lives.

We may find immense satisfaction in fostering and sharing the happiness of others. We may be satisfied knowing that we have supplied for those who are most important to us. We may be certain that our hard-earned money will not only provide for us in our old age but will also benefit others. We will always feel more meaningful and fulfilled when we contribute or offer our skills and abilities to help others. What we do with our money is about more than simply the dollars and cents; it's about the overall impact it may have.

If you've made it this far, you've probably realized that "true happiness" does not derive from materialistic pleasures. To truly envision what life would be like if we stopped pursuing materialism and instead lived in a meaningful and fulfilling way, consider what you would do if you had all the money in the world, and how you would use your financial affluence to affect change, assist a population or organization that is important to you, or advance a cause that wants to make the world a more helpful and equitable place. If we want to live a meaningful and fulfilling life, we must begin to focus our aims and energy on others.

www.ingramcontent.com/pod-product-compliance
Lightning Source LLC
Chambersburg PA
CBHW050253230526
45470CB00005B/2238